PRESENTED TO

_____

FROM

_____

DATE

_____

My Faithful Companion

H. NORMAN WRIGHT | ARTWORK BY JOHN WEISS

HARVEST HOUSE PUBLISHERS

EUGENE, OREGON

MY FAITHFUL COMPANION

Text Copyright © 2009 by H. Norman Wright.
Artwork Copyright by John Weiss,
licensed by The Greenwich Workshop, Inc.
www.greenwichworkshop.com.

Published by Harvest House Publishers
Eugene, Oregon 97402
www.harvesthousepublishers.com

ISBN 978-0-7369-2327-9

Cover by Koechel Peterson & Associates, Inc., Minneapolis, Minnesota

Printed in Hong Kong

09 10 11 12 13 14 15 16 17 / NG / 10 9 8 7 6 5 4 3 2 1

Contents

The Dog's in Charge 5

Pedro, the Fisherman.. 6

A Dog Named Lucy 10

Dogs Rule 13

Dog Questions 14

Casey's Lesson 19

The Morning Routine 23

Dogs in Heaven?.. 26

Losing Things.. 28

How *Not* to Train Your Puppy 31

The Dog Pound Syndrome 37

Sammy's Big Smile 38

You Can't Fool Your Dog 40

Going on a Trip Without Taking the Pack 43

A Dog's Nose Knows 44

Reunited 51

Hero Dogs 55

The dog was
created especially
for children.
He is the god
of the frolic.

HENRY WARD BEECHER

A dog can express more with his tail in minutes
than his owner can express with his tongue in hours.

ANONYMOUS

The Dog's in Charge

MY NAME IS SHADOW. No, I'm not named after any other dog. My owner (well, he thinks he's my owner!) just happened to choose this name over "Amadeus." Boy, am I thankful for that switch. Who wants to be named after a weird musician?

Anyway, I'm a golden retriever. I'm good-looking, in good shape, have a sweet personality, am obedient…you know, the all-around ideal dog.

My owner or my master (whatever he's called) lives under the impression that he has trained me. Now, I don't want to wag my own tail here, but the truth must be told: I've trained *him*. Let's look at some of the myths I hear him telling his friends. He's had the audacity to tell crowds of people that he's trained me to sit, stay, lie down, fetch the paper (boy, is that boring!), bring my leash, bring the food dish, chase the cat…you know the routine.

Boy, does Norm have it wrong. I trained him to say certain words or give certain gestures so that I can live comfortably and contentedly. That's right—I pick up the paper and he says, "Fetch. Good dog. Thank you." (I love the praise and attention.) I bring my leash to him and he takes me for a walk. I bring my dish and he feeds me. Every time I offer up what I want or need in this way, he obediently complies. It's a great arrangement. Could I convince him that this is truly how things work? Not in a thousand years, but that's all right. Let him live in darkness. Why fix what isn't broken? I just wanted to set the record straight so you know—the dog's in charge.

The most affectionate creature in the world is a wet dog.

Ambrose Bierce

Pedro, the Fisherman

The most touching dog story I've heard was told to me thirty years ago by a neighbor on her return from a Mediterranean cruise.

The setting of the story is a little cove on the east side of the Spanish island of Mallorca. It was there that an Englishman, a professional diver, lived on his yacht with his dog, a springer spaniel. He had tied his yacht to a pier where diving conditions were ideal. Each time the Englishman made a dive, the dog sat anxiously on the pier, awaiting his return. One day the dog became so concerned when the Englishman disappeared into the water that he dove in after him.

Underwater, the dog saw a school of fish swim past. He grabbed a fish and carried it back to the pier. The Englishman, surprised and pleased, praised him. After that, the dog followed the man on his dives. In the course of the shared diving, the dog developed excellent fishing skills, to the man's considerable amusement. The Englishman told the island's residents of his dog's accomplishments, and they came to the pier to watch. Delighted, they began calling the dog Pedro, after Peter, the fisherman.

One day the Englishman became ill, and shortly thereafter he died. Various townspeople tried to adopt Pedro, but the dog would never leave the beach for fear he would miss his master's return. He waited on the beach through hot sun and driving rain. People tried to feed him, but eventually they gave up. He wouldn't accept food from anyone other than his master. Finally, to feed himself, Pedro went back to fishing.

It happened that on this same island there were a number of stray cats. Ravenous, they would gather to watch Pedro dive into the schools of fish, select the fish he wanted, and bring it back to eat on the shore. Then the cats would fight over what the dog had left uneaten. The dog must have observed this, for one morning when Pedro had eaten his fill, he dove into the water again and came back up with a large fish, which he placed on the sand before the group of cats. Then he backed off and watched. One black cat, with greater courage than the others, approached the fish, grabbed it, and ran. After that, in addition to keeping vigil for his master, the dog also seemed to consider it his duty to feed those less fortunate. Every morning thereafter, Pedro the fisherman shared his catch with the hungry cats of Mallorca.[1]

Bob Toren

Dogs love company.
They place it first
in their short list
of needs.

J.R. ACKERLEY

Why It's Great to Be a Dog

1. No one cares if you spend hours a day just smelling things.

2. Every garbage can looks like a buffet.

3. People consider your wet nose to be a sign of good health.

4. You don't have to take a bath every day, and no one expects you to brush your own hair.

5. You never have to pay for dinner.

6. If you gain weight or have rotten table manners, it's someone else's fault.

7. No one is offended if you scratch in public.

The average dog has one request
to all humankind.
Love me.

HELEN EXLEY

A DOG NAMED LUCY

Lucy, I envy your one-pointed attention.
Never seeming to do two things at once,
  how do you get everything done?

I learned long ago to do several things at once.
My parents taught me through example:
  Dad could
      sit at the dinner table,
      eat,
      read the newspaper, always the funnies first, and
      and carry on a conversation all at the same time.
  Mom always listened to the radio and glanced at
  the mirror, no matter what else she was doing.

I can't help but
  read while I eat,
  read while I use the bathroom,
  listen to the radio while I drive (and drink coffee),
  glance at the newspaper when I talk to someone,
  drink coffee as I do therapy.

One of the happiest sights in the world comes
when a lost dog is reunited with a master he loves.
You just haven't seen joy till you have seen that.

ELDON ROARK

10

Do you get distracted, too, Lucy?
    Do you fantasize about your pal Remington while
        playing ball?
    Do you dream of bones lost and balls found while
        you hold a sit-stay?

Do dogs worry about
    death,
    vision loss,
    hearing loss,
    incontinence,
    cancer,
    poverty?

Who is going to take care of you in old age?
    Will you experience doctor-assisted suicide without
        even asking for it?
    Where are you going when you die?

Or are you always here in the present,
    alert to the opportunity for food,
    the chance to go for a walk,
    for someone to pet you?

Teach me one-pointed attention, Lucy;
    I long to be here fully, too.

For me, being fully present is tough;
I may be in one place, but my mind is often
    somewhere else—
        in the future,
        in the past,
        in daydreams—just not here.[2]

Dogs Rule

*For me a house
or an apartment
becomes a home
when you add
one set of four legs,
a happy tail,
and that indescribable
measure of love
that we call a dog.*

Roger Caras

HI. MY NAME IS REX. Yeah, I know…it's a pretty typical name for a dog, but it's better than some people names I've heard. Hate to break it to you, but I agree with Shadow. Every dog worth his kibble knows that he needs to train up his owner in order to live the good dog life. So many people think that a dog's bag of tricks only consists of begging and rolling over or playing dead. But there's so much more! I, as a faithful companion, make the relationship with you, a dog owner, go smoothly. Here's how…

Do I have to make sure I'm home at a certain time to feed you? Ha, that's a joke. But I've seen you change your schedule or come tearing into the driveway after work just to make sure I'm fed.

Do I take you outside after each meal to walk and potty? Go ahead—try to remember. And do you catch me picking up your droppings in a little sack? I don't think so—I have pride, after all. Just think about it. You—a human in your pressed, pinstripe suit or a designer dress—follow a dog around saying, "Go poo poo! Squat!" and then pick it up and carry it around the neighborhood for everyone to see. Yuk!

I dictate which car you use and the type of covering placed on the seat. And I even limit the amount of time you can shop when you leave me in the car.

For any relationship to be harmonious, for two beings to be compatible companions, there is one thing that must take place—compromise. So here it is: I'll pretend you're in charge if you keep on loving me like you do. Shake on it.

DOG QUESTIONS

Q: Why do dogs jump up to greet people?

A: From a dog's point of view, a better question is, "Why don't humans walk on all fours like just about every other animal and meet me at my level?"

An untrained dog will try to connect instinctively, and that means starting the greetings by jumping up for a closer whiff of human breath…Dogs have to be trained in human etiquette, and a lot of times we don't do a very good job of it.

Q: Why do dogs cock their heads when they hear unusual sounds?

A: A dog will tip his head to bring one ear forward, so he can better focus on the source of an unusual sound or a favorite one ("Cookie?"). Typically, these unusual sounds are high-pitched noises, such as squeaks. That makes sense, when you consider that many dogs will happily catch a rodent if the situation presents itself.

Q: Is a dog's mouth really cleaner that a human's?

A: We're sorry but…yuk! You don't have to be an oral hygiene expert to know that any animal who eats cat poop, horse doo, and garbage isn't exactly going to have a clean mouth. It's hard to imagine how such an idea ever got started, especially when you consider that we humans routinely floss and brush our teeth, gargle, visit the dentist, and worry about germs that cause bad breath.

So is a dog's mouth cleaner than a human's? Not at all![3]

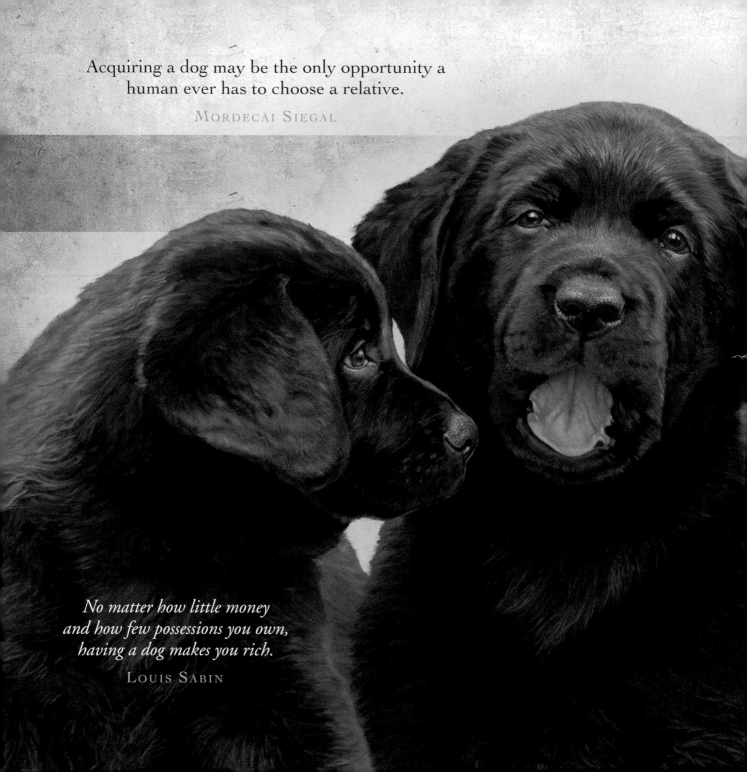

Acquiring a dog may be the only opportunity a
human ever has to choose a relative.

MORDECAI SIEGAL

*No matter how little money
and how few possessions you own,
having a dog makes you rich.*

LOUIS SABIN

Dogs never lie about love.

JEFFREY MOUSSAIEFF MASSON

Dog ownership is like a rainbow.
Puppies are the joy at one end.
Old dogs are the treasure at the other.

CAROLYN ALEXANDER

Casey's Lesson

SOME SHELTIES see no reason to acknowledge the presence of anyone other than their chosen person, except to warn them. So I was shocked when one day my sheltie, Casey, joyfully ran up to an elderly couple he did not know. He danced about and cuddled up for their attention, ignoring me as I called for him to come back.

After that incident, I began carefully watching Casey's behavior with other people. Casey didn't care for strangers who were in their twenties, thirties, or forties, and he even ran away from children, but let someone with gray hair walk by, and Casey ran to greet them enthusiastically. Since this was not typical sheltie behavior, I began to think that maybe Casey was intended to accomplish something greater with his life. And maybe I could help him.

I contacted my church's nursing home and found out that they let dogs visit the residents. I felt confident Casey could brighten the day for many of the people at this facility, but I was uncertain how I could handle taking him there. Most of the residents in this nursing home were Alzheimer's patients. How could Casey and I communicate with them?

The minute Casey stepped into the nursing home, people greeted us with smiles and laughter.

Casey happily did his tricks for them. After Casey finished entertaining the patients, he wagged his tail, cuddled up, and listened to his elders, especially when they called him "pretty dog." Casey accepted every hand that reached out to him with a friendly lick and wag of his tail.

The next thing I knew, people who couldn't tell where they were or even who they were would glow with a light in their eyes and reminisce about the dogs they had loved. When a nurse saw that one old gent had started talking to Casey, she pulled me aside and whispered, "He hasn't said a word since he got here—until now!"

Someone else asked me to take Casey to a woman who was unable to move from her bed or even speak. As the woman petted Casey's head and hummed at him, I observed indications of a sharp and active mind behind her bright eyes. She happily responded to my questions with a nod or an elegant wave of her hand.

I left the nursing home that day feeling very grateful to Casey for the lesson he had taught me. I had been afraid to step outside the boundaries I had placed around myself and worried about how I would communicate with these people. But I learned that no one ever forgets the language of love.[4]

You may have a dog that won't sit up,
roll over or even cook breakfast, not because she's too stupid to learn how
but because she's too smart to bother.

RICK HOROWITZ, COLUMNIST

REMEMBER

Dogs and cats are better than kids because they:

1. Eat less
2. Don't ask for money all the time
3. Are easier to train
4. Normally come when called
5. Never ask to drive the car
6. Don't hang out with drug-using friends
7. Don't smoke or drink
8. Don't have to buy the latest fashions
9. Don't want to wear your clothes
10. Don't need a gazillion dollars for college

AUTHOR UNKNOWN

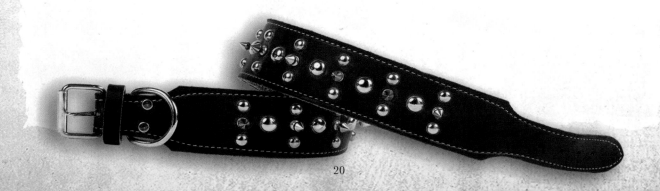

The Morning Routine

IT'S EARLY in the morning. You're lying on your side with your eyes closed, enjoying the quiet and the solitude. Gradually you open them, and to your shock you're staring into another set of eyes behind a huge nose just four inches from your face. And now that you're awake, a large, wet tongue lashes out to wash your face. This is "good morning" in dog lingo. Aren't dogs wonderful? They're there to greet us first thing in the morning, and they can even serve as an alarm clock. Wow!

A dog has the ability to wake us out of the deepest sleep in the most obnoxious ways. We've already identified the "wet tongue approach." Another is the "flying leap." Your dog, whether ten pounds or one hundred fifty pounds, takes a calculated flying leap from the middle of the floor to the middle of the bed. Does he care what portion of your anatomy he lands on? Not in the least. You awaken with a start and check to make sure your body is still in one piece and functional.

Isn't it great to be loved by your dog?

The "probing paw" is another favorite. A probing paw keeps hitting you over and over. You keep batting it away, but it's more persistent than you are. There is no letup and it strikes your body again and again. The only recourse is open your eyes, get out of bed, and either feed him or take him out to potty or both.

"Panting" right next to your head is yet another effective technique. In your comatose state, you hear this sound somewhat like a train in the distance. It seems to increase in volume. As you start to surface, you realize it's not a train barreling through town in the distance, but it's panting...and behind the panting is that obnoxious odor of...dog breath. Oh, you can plug your ears and hold your nose, but a "panter" personality won't leave. After all, you are his. You belong to him—your dog. And no matter what method he uses, it's his special way of saying, "Hi there. I missed you during the night, and I want to see you. I love you."

Each breed of dog has its own unique set of characteristics and personality traits that make it special. For instance:

◇ An Airedale believes that it is of no use to anyone unless it provokes a furor.

◇ Each year, a healthy Jack Russell terrier consumes one and a half times his weight in human patience.

◇ Bulldogs display that typically English characteristic for which there is no English name.

◇ All poodles act as if they have won first prize in the lottery of life.

◇ All spaniels have a way of getting the answer "yes" without ever having posed any clear question.

◇ The Chihuahua's greatest ambition is to live in a hot country and watch its master throw stones in the sea.

◇ Golden retrievers are not dogs—they are a form of catharsis.

◇ The beautiful and elegant Afghan hound knows two things:
    First, it is not very smart.
    Second, it doesn't matter.[5]

Inside every Newfoundland, Boxer, Elkhound,
and Great Dane is a puppy
longing to climb on to your lap.

HELEN THOMSON

Dogs in Heaven?

ARE THERE DOGS in heaven? For those who love dogs, it would be the worst form of a lie to call any place where dogs were banned "Paradise." Certainly no loving God would separate people from their canine friends for eternity.

Robert Louis Stevenson, author of novels such as *Treasure Island*, declared, "You think dogs will not be in heaven? I tell you, they will be there before any of us." George Eliot, the English writer of *Middlemarch* and *Adam Bede*, asked, "Shall we, because we walk on our hind feet, assume to ourselves only the privilege of imperishability? Shall we, who are even as they, though we wag our tongues and not our tails, demand a special Providence and a selfish salvation?"

Then there was Saint Patrick, the patron saint of Ireland. Tradition says that he promised Oissain, the son of the great hero Finn Mac-Cumhail, that for helping him Christianize the land he could have the hounds in heaven.

Martin Luther, founder of the Protestant church, was once asked by a child whether her dog would be allowed in heaven. He gently patted the dog's head and said, "Be comforted, little dog. Thou too in the Resurrection shalt have a tail of gold."

I had a dream shortly after my old cairn terrier, Flint, died. In it Flint was lying beside the gates of heaven, and an angel came out to ask him why he didn't come in. In the telepathic speech common to celestial beings, my dog answered, "Can't I just stay out here awhile? I'll be good and I won't even bark. You see, I'm waiting for someone that I miss very much. If I went in alone, it wouldn't be heaven for me." I woke from that dream to find tears on my face.[6]

A good dog never dies,
he always stays,
he walks beside you on
crisp autumn days when
frost is on the fields and
winter's drawing near,
his head is within our
hand in his old way.

MARY CAROLYN DAVIES

LOSING THINGS

Do you ever lose things?

I've seen you hunt for a tennis ball,
        but you do not obsess.
        You give up and go to your pillow.

Not I.

I've spent a total of 14 years,
        three months,
        three days,
        and three hours so far,
        searching for lost stuff.

How could I be so dumb as to have misplaced that
        check, wallet, watch, glasses, keys, phone slip,
        notebook, tape, ring, knife, toy, blanket, glove,
        sock, medicine bottle, paper, book, hat…

My idea of heaven is a pile of my lost stuff
        —a lot of good it will do me there.

Better to think I'll ultimately find all the answers
        to my most perplexing questions

        —like how much do dogs know?[7]

It's no coincidence that man's best friend cannot talk.

ANONYMOUS

Say something idiotic and nobody
but a dog politely wags his tail.

Virginia Graham
Everything's Too Something

How *NOT* to Train Your Puppy

"I'M HAVING TROUBLE paper-training my puppy," said the distressed female voice on the other end of the line.

This is a common city problem, so I leaned back in the chair, prepared for a friendly, if oft-told, fifteen minutes. "What seems to be the problem?" I asked absentmindedly.

"She just isn't getting it. Every morning, I get up and show her what to do, but she just isn't catching on."

"Show her?" I swung my legs off the desk, sitting up. "You mean that you go—"

"Yes, every morning. She still doesn't get it. Is she dumb?" the voice asked earnestly.

"Whoa…" I began, now completely engaged. My mind was racing. Did she do this in her bathrobe, hiking it up? Or maybe she dressed first? I was torn—laugh or be professional? Professional won.

"Dogs don't normally learn by watching," I said in a studied, calm tone. "If they did, they would dial out for pizza and run up our credit cards ordering squeaky toys."

From that point on we made some real headway in both paper-training and limiting this poor woman's morning mess. Bless the devoted, if confused, owner. Her heart was in the right place, just not the rest of her.

Sarah and I figure she has to live alone. We just could not imagine the conversations if she were married. "Ah…sweetheart, what are you doing?"[8]

YOU KNOW YOU'RE A DOG LOVER WHEN...

- your dog licks your food but you eat it anyway.

- you spell out words like "walk" and "treat" even when you're talking to humans.

- your dog has a toy box that's so stuffed it won't close.

- you and your dog go for car rides just so he can stick his head out the window.

- you've left parties or other social gatherings to go home and feed your dog.

- your dog has eaten off your dishes more than your guests have.

- you buy a king-sized bed so there's room for your dogs.

- your dog drinks from the toilet, but you let him kiss you anyway.

- you buy your dog a Happy Meal at McDonald's (hey—he likes the toy!).

- you've always got a plastic bag on hand—just in case.

*No one can fully understand
love unless he is owned by a dog.*

GENE HILL

The dog is the most faithful of animals
and would be much esteemed
were it not so common.
Our Lord God has made
His greatest gift the commonest.

MARTIN LUTHER

The dog has seldom
pulled man up to his level
of sagacity,
but man has frequently
dragged the dog
down to his.

JAMES THURBER

35

I am joy in a wooly coat,
come to dance into your life,
to make you laugh!

JULIE CHURCH

The Dog Pound Syndrome

THE "DOG POUND" is an old term—one that conjures up negative images and memories. We have other names today for the same facilities. But who would ever think that phrase would have a usage in the world of dating and possible matrimony.

My friend was widowed, and after a number of months of grieving was quite lonely. He really wanted to find some female companionship and perhaps even someone to marry. He remembered a woman he liked more than fifty years ago who was a friend to both him and his now-deceased wife. He tracked her down. She lived in a different city, so they began a correspondence. Soon they were talking an hour a day on the phone. Next flights back and forth commenced, and they became almost inseparable. It looked promising. One day he said to me, "Norm, we had a discussion the other night. Since this relationship has moved ahead so fast and intense, we decided that we want to make sure this is the real thing and not the 'dog pound' syndrome." I looked at him and said, "What in the world is the 'dog pound' syndrome?" "Well, you know that if you're a dog in the pound and you've been there a while, you know that in a few days your time is up and you're going to be toast. So the first person that comes in and shows you any interest at all, no matter if they smell, they're ugly, a deviant, or can't talk straight, they're the greatest person on earth and you'll love them forever if they'll just get you out of this pound. It doesn't matter who they are; they're your savior."

I said, "Warren, you didn't say this to her?"

"Yup. We both agreed we needed to make sure this wasn't us."

Sammy's Big Smile

My Aunt Julie had a dog named Sammy, a little black Chihuahua mix with a tongue as long as her body…This adorable black dog always greeted you with a "doggy smile." Sammy owned my Aunt Julie, and everyone in our family knew it.

One afternoon I was visiting my aunt. We were all dressed up and going out. I don't remember the occasion, but I do remember that we were in an awful rush…Sammy, however, wasn't in any rush. The only thing Sammy was interested in was getting some attention.

"No, Sammy, we cannot play," my aunt scolded, "We have to go! *Now!*"

The problem was that we couldn't go because Aunt Julie had misplaced her false teeth. The longer we searched for her teeth…the more attention Sammy seemed to demand. We ignored Sammy's barking, as we looked frantically for the missing dentures.

Finally, Aunt Julie reached her breaking point and gave up. She plunked herself down at the bottom of the stairs and cried… At that moment, Sammy gave a few shrill barks, this time from the top of the stairs, and then was quiet. As we turned around to see what she wanted, we both exploded into laughter. There stood a "smiling" Sammy—with Aunt Julie's false teeth in her mouth—her tail wagging a hundred miles an hour. The message in her sparkling eyes was obvious: *I've been trying to tell you for a half hour—I know where your teeth are!*

GAYLE DELHAGEN
One of the Family

You Can't Fool Your Dog

THE HOUSE IS QUIET. Your dog is asleep in the other part of the house. Your mouth waters at the thought of that last piece of cake in the kitchen. You rise from the chair slowly and slip off your shoes to walk quietly to the kitchen. You approach the cupboard and with both hands you gently, gradually open it. Without a sound, without releasing a breath, you reach for the cake, lift it out, turn around, and…

There he is!

How did he know? You were like a stealth plane—yet he knew, and he's sitting there with that expression, "So…cake, huh? Were you planning to share or were you going to eat it all by yourself? Aren't you going to share with your faithful companion? Huh…huh?" Fool your dog? Right!

Your dog loves to ride. He runs to the door, jumps up and down with excitement, and you both climb into the car. But today you can't take him, so to avoid the pain and agony of leaving your furry friend behind, you decide to sneak out. You nonchalantly put your hand over your keys, gripping them tightly so they don't make a noise, while at the same time you slap a magazine on the counter with your other hand to distract your dog. Your hand holds and hides the keys as you wander around the room, working your way toward the back door, whistling and looking so relaxed and casual. You're going to pull it off! You make a slight diversion into another room and then tiptoe toward the back door. Just as you congratulate yourself for being so smart…

There he is!

With leash in mouth, he's looking at you with eyes that say, "What took you so long? Let's go!" Fool your dog? Right!

If you think dogs can't count,
try putting three dog biscuits in your pocket
and then giving Fido only two of them.

PHIL PASTORET, AUTHOR

If you don't own a dog, at least one,
there is not necessarily
anything wrong with you,
but there may be something
wrong with your life.

ROGER CARAS, *A Celebration of Dogs*

Going on a Trip Without Taking the Pack

DOGS CAN SENSE IT. Before you've booked your flight online or routed a journey on the map, a dog knows you're going on a trip, and she knows when it's one that you're taking without her. But instead of enjoying the time she has with you before departure day, she starts to act up and act out. The solution? Don't let her know.

Make your travel arrangements when your dog is out of earshot. Better yet, make them when you are miles away in your car or at the office. Then, days in advance, while your dog is enjoying her afternoon nap outside in the sun, pull the blinds and get out the suitcases from the garage or hall closet. Put them in your bedroom and shut the door. Start to select clothes and toiletries to pack, but only when she's outside. This could take several days of well-timed effort.

Don't ever talk about the trip in front of her. Act normal. Take all calls relevant to your trip while in another room or outside. Yawn in your dog's presence. Be yourself—except even more casual. And be an extra-diligent homebody. Hang out in the evenings and sit on the porch swing for long stretches as though you'd never, ever consider leaving.

Will all this work? Absolutely not.

Dogs know. We don't know how they know, but they do. We might be as careful and secretive as a spy, but when change is a-comin' or we're a-goin', our canine companions have a way of knowing. While all we want to do is pack in peace, their heart's desire is to keep the pack together. Isn't that why we hate saying goodbye?

> Don't accept your dog's admiration as conclusive
> evidence that you are wonderful.
>
> ANN LANDERS

A DOG'S NOSE KNOWS

ANGELA IS A YOUNG high school girl who is quadriplegic and has seizures. She acquired her first therapy dog at the age of 11. Her current golden retriever service dog, Harley, is quite large and highly intelligent as was Hershey, the first one. He's able to detect when she is about to have a seizure, alerts her in advance, and then keeps her immobilized. The seizures used to last 90 seconds, but now most of them are 3-9 seconds. Everyone in the family has learned to take their cues from the dog and learn what his responses mean rather than trying to teach him certain ways of responding. Harley also knows when something is wrong with her, and when she can't respond he hits an emergency button and then emergency workers come on the intercom. Angela can then describe what is wrong, but if she can't and they hear a bark, they're on their way.

He is not only able to alert his owner of an impending seizure but can also detect cancer and other things through smelling.

One day when Angela was getting on her bus to go to school with her dog she looked at her dog and then at the bus driver and just blurted out to the driver, "Are you pregnant?" and the bus driver said, "No, I'm not pregnant." Her mother was a bit taken back by her bluntness and talked to her that evening. The next day when the bus arrived it came to a halt, the bus driver jumped off, looked for Angela, and said, "Guess what! I took a pregnancy test yesterday and discovered I'm expecting." Angela's dog had the ability to determine whether a woman was pregnant or not. He would go up to a woman, push his nose into her stomach, and his back would be in a straight line and his tail would be straight but then drop down, and that would be the indication that meant a woman was expecting.

To your dog, you are the greatest,
the smartest, the nicest
human being who was ever born.

LOUIS SABIN

Pet Rules

Dear Dogs and Cats,

The stairway was not designed by NASCAR and is not a racetrack. Beating me to the bottom is not the object. Tripping me doesn't help because I fall faster than you can run.

I cannot buy anything bigger than a king-sized bed. I am very sorry about this. Dogs and cats can actually curl up in a ball when they sleep. It is not necessary to sleep perpendicular, stretched out to the fullest extent possible. I also know that sticking tails straight out and having tongues hanging out the other end to maximize space is nothing but sarcasm.

For the last time, there is not a secret exit from the bathroom. If by some miracle I beat you there and manage to get the door shut, it is not necessary to claw, whine, meow, try to turn the knob, or get your paw under the edge and try to pull the door open. I must exit through the same door I entered. Also, I have been using the bathroom for years—canine or feline attendance is not required.

The proper order is kiss me and then go smell the other dog or cat's behind. I cannot stress this enough!

47

To pacify you, my dear pets,
I have posted the following message on our front door:

TO ALL NON–PET OWNERS
WHO VISIT AND
LIKE TO COMPLAIN
ABOUT OUR PETS:

1. They live here. You don't.

2. If you don't want their hair on your clothes,
stay off the furniture.
(That's why they call it "fur"niture.)

3. I like my pets a lot better than I like most people.

4. To you, it's an animal.
To me, he/she is an adopted son/daughter
who is short, hairy, walks on all fours,
and doesn't speak clearly.

The more I see of men,
the more I like dogs.

MADAME DE STAEL
18th century French activist

Reunited

KATRINA—a story of loss—the loss of homes, cars, a culture, people, and pets. So much was lost with very little recovered. Such was the case of Martha, who had lived in a small, older house in the Ninth Ward of New Orleans with her small dog, Fritz. One night the waters of the hurricane swept through aided by multiple breaks in the levee, and the floodwaters rose faster than anyone could imagine. Rescue workers came into Martha's house and moved her to a boat and safety. But in the panic Fritz was forgotten and left behind. It was a few hours later that it dawned on Martha that Fritz had not been rescued, as was the case with thousands of animals in that area. Not only did Martha lose her home and belongings, but also her only remaining family member, Fritz.

Six weeks later Martha stopped by our Victim Chaplain headquarters at the edge of the Ninth Ward. She wondered if someone could accompany her and take her back to what was left of her home to find Fritz's remains and bury him. The director of Victim Chaplain's said he would be happy to take her. They arrived, went up to the front door, opened it, and walked in. Then they heard the sound—a weak "woof" coming from the bathroom. Looking at one another in shock, they opened the door of the bathroom and there stood Fritz, skin and bones on legs barely able to hold him up. He had existed on water and chewing up anything edible in the confines of that room. He was just hours away from death, so they rushed him to a vet and IVs were started immediately. Today Martha doesn't have her old home, but she does have something more important—Fritz. It's an ending similar to a story in the New Testament about a father and a son. "This son of mine was dead and is alive again; he was lost and is found" (Luke 15:24). This father rejoiced and so did Martha.

Tell me, if you can, of anything that's finer than

an evening in camp with a rare old friend and a

dog after one's heart.

NASH BUCKINGHAM

I can't think of anything that brings me closer to tears than when my old dog —
completely exhausted after a hard day in the field —
limps away from her nice spot in front of the fire and comes over
to where I'm sitting and puts her head in my lap,
a paw over my knee, and closes her eyes, and goes back to sleep.
I don't know what I've done to deserve that kind of friend.

GENE HILL

Life is like a dogsled team:
If you ain't the lead dog,
the scenery never changes.

LEWIS GRIZZARD, HUMORIST

Then who shall picture the urgency of a boy,
running, awkwardly, with a great dog in his arms
running through the village,
past the empty mill, past the Labor Exchange,
where the men looked up from their deep
ponderings on life and the dole?
Or who shall describe the high tones
of a voice—a boy's voice,
calling as he runs up a path:
"Mother! Oh, mother! Lassie's come home!
Lassie's come home!

ERIC KNIGHT, *"Lassie Come-Home"*

*The one absolutely unselfish friend that man
can have in this selfish world,
the one that never deserts him,
the one that never proves ungrateful or treacherous,
is his dog.*

GEORGE GRAHAM VEST, *Eulogy on the Dogs*

HERO DOGS

Rigel

THE TRIP WAS going to be magnificent. Luxurious. Breathtaking. Its "who's who" passenger list included the wealthy—and, for many, their pets. In fact, had the *Titanic* not sunk in the wee hours of the morning on April 15, 1912, many of its first-class passengers would have been strutting their stuff at a dog show later in the day.

Most of the people—and animals—perished that fateful morning when the "unsinkable" ship went down. But several pets made it to safety, and one brave pooch earned itself safe passage to shore—and hero status to boot.

Rigel, a black Newfoundland, spent three hours swimming in the icy ocean until the rescue ship, *Carpathia*, arrived. The survivors crammed into one particular lifeboat were too exhausted to shout out a warning to the *Carpathia*, whose crew did not see them floating in the chilly waves below. But Rigel still had more than a spark of life left in him. Letting out a load bark, he alerted the rescue ship's captain to the presence of the survivors. And, continuing to swim ahead of the lifeboat, he led them to the ship's gangway.

Rigel's owner, the first officer of the *Titanic*, had gone down with his ship. But a sailor on the *Carpathia* was eager to adopt this resilient dog who had saved the lives of the terror-stricken and weary survivors of the great ship *Titanic*.

Barry

HE WAS A QUIET and unassuming inhabitant of a monastery in the mountains of Switzerland, but he chose his day of defiance well.

Barry the St. Bernard was accompanying a man through the mountains one day when an avalanche thundered into the region. The man fled for the monastery, but Barry refused to go back. Instead, the trained rescue dog did something he had never done before—he ran away.

Barry followed his nose to a young boy who was stranded on an icy ledge. As the snow continued to fall and cover the boy and his makeshift shelter, Barry carefully crawled up the ledge to reach him. Trained to revive those he rescued by warming them, the brave St. Bernard gently licked the boy's face. Awakened by the dog's actions, the grateful boy grabbed onto his furry rescuer's neck. Measuring each and every step, Barry negotiated his way down the ledge, his precious cargo clinging to him. The dog then headed for the monastery, where the astonished monks soon realized why their faithful charge hadn't immediately come home.

In the span of 15 years, Barry—who epitomized the gallantry and strength of the magnificent St. Bernard breed—was responsible for saving the lives of more than 40 people lost in the snowy peaks. He remains perhaps the greatest rescue dog the world has ever witnessed.

Dusty

DUSTY CAME FACE-TO-FACE with a new challenge, searching through the rubble at the World Trade Center. Despite no training for such a situation, he walked fearlessly across beams with 20-foot drops on either side. This type of search and rescue was all new to him, as his primary job had been tracking down bad guys. Now he was looking for the good guys. His eagerness to find someone kept him looking and digging. He found several, but none were alive. Unlike many other dogs, he never lost his eagerness for the search and never became depressed.

Dusty's greatest contribution, however, was providing comfort to the rescue workers. His presence seemed to help the rescue workers keep going day after day. Tough, quiet men would let their guard down with Dusty, and you could just see the stress leave their body when they wrapped their arms around this 100-pound dog. Many buried their heads in his fur to give expression to their pain and sorrow, and then they looked up with a smile.

Shadow

SHADOW WENT TO NEW YORK not as a search and rescue dog, but to provide comfort and stability to the rescue workers within days after 9/11. Shadow's approach to the workers was an invitation to come close to him. He would go to the person and touch his nose to their knee. If they responded he would give a wave with his paw and then put both paws on their legs. Who could resist that approach? As the person came closer, Shadow moved closer and then gave them a hug by putting his paws on their shoulders. Shadow leaned against those who were withdrawn until they responded.

Shadow and other dogs like him soon became known as "comfort" dogs. And many said, "Being with this dog is what got me through the day and the worst of times."

Let's always remember the victims of 9/11, their families, and those who responded.

NOTES

1. Bob Toren, "Pedro the Fisherman" from *Chicken Soup for the Dog Lover's Soul,* edited by Jack Canfield, Mark Victor Hansen, Marty Becker, D.V.M., Carol Kline, and Amy D. Shojai. Copyright © 2004 by Bob Toren. Reprinted with the permission of Health Communications, Inc., www.hcibooks.com.

2. Robert Pasick, Ph.D., *Conversations with My Old Dog* (Center City, MN: Hazelden, 2000), pp. 2-3; www.leadersconnect.com. Reprinted with permission.

3. Marty Becker, D.V.M., and Gina Spadafori, excerpts from *Why Do Dogs Drink Out of the Toilet?* Copyright © 2006 by Marty Becker and Gina Spadafori. Reprinted with the permission of Health Communications, Inc., www.hcibooks.com.

4. From the book *Angel Dogs.* Copyright © 2005 by Allen and Linda Anderson. Reprinted with permission of New World Library, Novato, CA. www.newworldlibrary.com.

5. Reprinted with the permission of The Free Press, a division of Simon & Schuster Adult Publishing Group, from *What Do Dogs Know?* by Stanley Coren and Janet Walker. Copyright © 1993 by Stanley Coren and Janet Walker. All rights reserved.

6. Ibid.

7. Pasick, *Conversations,* p. 19.

8. Brian Kilcommons and Sarah Wilson, *Tails from the Bark Side* (New York, NY: Warner Books, 1997), pp. 144-45.

Some quotes were selected from *The Quotable Dog,* compiled by Greg Snider (New York, NY: McGraw-Hill, 1994).